PSYC

A joint projec

of the

Education Directorate

and the

Office of Public Communications

The American Psychological Association

Washington, DC

2000

IENTIFIC PROBLEM SOLVERS

CAREERS FOR THE TWENTY-FIRST CENTURY

OLOGY

The many specialized interests of psychologists are represented through APA's divisions. Below are the names and **numbers** *of APA's active divisions.*

Addictions /**50**
Adult Development and Aging /**20**
American Psychology-Law Society /**41**
Applied Experimental and Engineering Psychology /**21**
Behavioral Neuroscience and Comparative Psychology /**6**
Child, Youth, and Family Services /**37**
Clinical Child Psychology (Division 12, Section I) /**53**
Clinical Neuropsychology /**40**
Consulting Psychology /**13**
Counseling Psychology /**17**
Developmental Psychology /**7**
Educational Psychology /**15**
Evaluation, Measurement, and Statistics /**5**
Exercise and Sport Psychology /**47**
Experimental Analysis of Behavior /**25**
Experimental Psychology /**3**
Family Psychology /**43**
Group Psychology and Group Psychotherapy /**49**
Health Psychology /**38**
History of Psychology /**26**
Humanistic Psychology /**32**
International Psychology /**52**
Media Psychology /**46**
Mental Retardation and Developmental Disabilities /**33**
Military Psychology /**19**
Peace Psychology /**48**
Population and Environmental Psychology /**34**
Psychoanalysis /**39**
Psychological Hypnosis /**30**
Psychologists in Independent Practice /**42**
Psychologists in Public Service /**18**
Psychology and the Arts /**10**
Psychology of Religion /**36**
Psychopharmacology and Substance Abuse /**28**
Psychotherapy /**29**
Rehabilitation Psychology /**22**
School Psychology /**16**
Society for Community Research and Action: Division of Community Psychology /**27**
Society for Consumer Psychology /**23**
Society for General Psychology /**1**
Society for Industrial and Organizational Psychology /**14**
Society for Personality and Social Psychology /**8**
Society for the Psychological Study of Ethnic Minority Issues /**45**
Society for the Psychological Study of Lesbian, Gay, and Bisexual Issues /**44**
Society for the Psychological Study of Men and Masculinity /**51**
Society for the Psychological Study of Social Issues /**9**
Society for the Psychology of Women /**35**
Society for the Teaching of Psychology /**2**
Society of Clinical Psychology /**12**
Society of Pediatric Psychology (Division 12, Section V) /**54**
State Psychological Association Affairs /**31**
Theoretical and Philosophical Psychology /**24**

CONTENTS

WHAT PSYCHOLOGY IS

Why people do the things they do is an age-old question. However, psychology—the science concerned with behavior, both humans and animals—is only about 125 years old. Despite its youth, it is a broad discipline, essentially spanning subject matter from biology to sociology. Biology studies the structures and functions of living organisms. Sociology examines how groups function in society. Psychologists study two critical relationships: one between brain function and behavior, and one between the environment and behavior. As scientists, psychologists follow scientific methods, using careful observation, experimentation, and analysis. But psychologists also need to be creative in the way they apply scientific findings.

Psychologists are frequently innovators, evolving new approaches from established knowledge to meet changing needs of people and societies. They develop theories and test them through their research. As this research yields new information, these findings become part of the body of knowledge that practitioners call on in their work with clients and patients. Psychology is a tremendously varied field. Psychologists conduct both basic and applied research, serve as consultants to communities and organizations, diagnose and treat people, and teach future psychologists and other types of students. They test intelligence and personality. They assess behavioral and mental function and well-being, stepping in to help where appropriate. They study how human beings relate to each other and also to machines, and they work to improve these relationships. And with America undergoing large changes in its population makeup, psychologists bring important knowledge and skills to understanding diverse cultures.

Many psychologists work independently. They also team up with other professionals—for example, other scientists, physicians, lawyers, school personnel, computer experts, engineers, policymakers, and managers—to contribute to every area of society. Thus we find them in laboratories, hospitals, courtrooms, schools and universities, community health centers, prisons, and corporate offices.

Psychologists traditionally study both normal and abnormal functioning, and also treat patients with mental and emotional problems. Today, they are increasingly concentrating on behaviors that affect the mental and emotional health and mental processes of healthy human beings. For example, they work with business executives, performers, and athletes to combat stress and improve performance. They advise lawyers on jury selection and collaborate with educators on school reform. They show up immediately following a disaster, such as a plane crash or bombing, to help victims and bystanders recover from the trauma, or shock, of the event. They team with law enforcement and public health officials to analyze the causes of such events and prevent their occurrence. Involved in all aspects of our fast-paced world, psychologists must keep up with what's happening all around us. When you're a psychologist, your education never ends.

Psychology is a discipline with a bright future. Among fields requiring a college degree, it is expected to be the third fastest-growing field in America through the year 2005 and to continue to grow steadily for at least another dozen years after that.

Opportunities for work in psychology are expanding in number and scope. The move toward preventing illness, rather than merely diagnosing and treating it, requires people to learn how to make healthy behavior a routine part of living. Indeed, many of the problems facing society today are problems about behavior, for example, drug addiction, poor personal relationships, violence at home and in the street, and the harm we do to our environment. Psychologists contribute solutions to problems through careful collection of data, analysis of data, and development of intervention strategies—in other words, by applying scientific principles, the hallmark of psychology.

In addition, an aging America is leading to more research and practice in adapting our homes and workplaces for older people. The promises of the electronic revolution demand more user-friendly technologies and training. More women in the workplace calls for employers to accommodate the needs of families. Psychologists are helping employers to make the changes that are needed. The diversity of America today calls for psychologists to develop and refine therapies to meet the unique needs of different ethnic groups. Furthermore, research advances in learning and memory, and the integration of physical and mental health care, make psychology more exciting than ever.

Most psychologists say they love their work. They cite the variety from day to day and the flexibility of their schedules. They are thrilled by the exciting changes taking place in the field, from working with primary care physicians to using computers. Most of all, they are committed to helping people manage the ups and downs of daily life.

The study of psychology is also good preparation for many other professions. Many employers are interested in the skills that psychology majors bring to collecting, analyzing, and interpreting data, and their experience with statistics and experimental design.

SOME OF THE SUBFIELDS IN PSYCHOLOGY

Psychologists specialize in a host of different areas within the field and identify themselves by many different labels. A sampling of those focal areas is presented to give you an idea of the breadth of psychology's content as well as the many different settings in which it is found. Additionally, many psychologists teach psychology in academic institutions from high schools to graduate programs in universities.

The field of psychology encompasses both research, through which we learn fundamental things about human and animal behavior, and practice, through which that knowledge is applied in helping to solve human problems. In each of the subfields there are psychologists who work primarily as researchers, others who work primarily as practitioners, and many who do both (scientist-practitioners). Indeed, one of psychology's most unique and important characteristics is its coupling of science and practice, which stimulates continual advancement of both.

Clinical psychologists assess and treat mental, emotional, and behavioral disorders. These range from short-term crises, such as difficulties resulting from adolescent rebellion, to more severe, chronic conditions such as schizophrenia.

Some clinical psychologists treat specific problems exclusively, such as phobias or clinical depression. Others focus on specific populations: youngsters, ethnic minority groups, gays and lesbians, and the elderly, for instance.

Counseling psychologists help people to accommodate to change or to make changes in their lifestyle. For example, they provide vocational and career assessment and guidance or help someone come to terms with the death of a loved one. They help students adjust to college, and people to stop smoking or overeating. They also consult with physicians on physical problems that have underlying psychological causes.

Developmental psychologists study the psychological development of the human being that takes place throughout life. Until recently, the primary focus was on childhood and adolescence, the most formative years. But as life expectancy in this country approaches 80 years, developmental psychologists are becoming increasingly interested in aging, especially in researching and developing ways to help elderly people stay as independent as possible.

Educational psychologists concentrate on how effective teaching and learning take place. They consider a variety of factors, such as human abilities, student motivation, and the effect on the classroom of the diversity of race, ethnicity, and culture that makes up America.

Engineering psychologists conduct research on how people work best with machines. For example, how can a computer be designed to prevent fatigue and eye strain? What arrangement of an assembly line makes production most efficient? What is a reasonable workload? Most engineering psychologists work in industry, but some are employed by the government, particularly the Department of Defense. They are often known as human factors specialists.

Forensic psychologists apply psychological principles to legal issues. Their expertise is often essential in court. They can, for example, help a judge decide which parent should have custody of a child or evaluate a defendant's mental competence to stand trial. Some forensic psychologists are trained in both psychology and the law.

Health psychologists are interested in how biological, psychological, and social factors affect health and illness. They identify the kinds of medical treatment people seek and get; how patients handle illness; why some people don't follow medical advice; and the most effective ways to control pain or to change poor health habits. They also develop health care strategies that foster emotional and physical well-being.

Psychologists team up with medical personnel in private practice and in hospitals to provide patients with complete health care. They educate medical staff about psychological problems that arise from the pain and stress of illness and about symptoms that may seem to be physical in origin but actually have psychological causes.

Health psychologists also investigate issues that affect a large segment of society, and develop and implement programs to deal with these problems. Examples are teenage pregnancy, substance abuse, risky sexual behaviors, smoking, lack of exercise, and poor diet.

continued

Industrial/organizational psychologists apply psychological principles and research methods to the work place in the interest of improving productivity and the quality of work life. Many serve as human resources specialists, helping organizations with staffing, training, and employee development and management in such areas as strategic planning, quality management, and coping with organizational change.

Neuropsychologists explore the relationships between brain systems and behavior. For example, neuropsychologists may study the way the brain creates and stores memories, or how various diseases and injuries of the brain affect emotion, perception, and behavior. Neuropsychologists frequently help design tasks to study normal brain functions with new imaging techniques, such as positron emission tomography (PET), single photon emission computed tomography (SPECT), and functional magnetic resonance imaging (FMRI).

Neuropsychologists also assess and treat people. And with the dramatic increase in the number of survivors of traumatic brain injury over the past 30 years, neuropsychologists are working with health teams to help brain-injured people resume productive lives.

Quantitative and measurement psychologists focus on methods and techniques for acquiring and analyzing psychological data. Some develop new methods for performing analysis; others create research strategies to assess the effect of social and educational programs and psychological treatment. They develop and evaluate mathematical models for psychological tests. They also propose methods for evaluating the quality and fairness of the tests.

Rehabilitation psychologists work with stroke and accident victims, people with mental retardation, and those with developmental disabilities caused by such conditions as cerebral palsy, epilepsy, and autism. They help clients adapt to their situation, frequently working with other health care professionals. They deal with issues of personal adjustment, interpersonal relations, the work world, and pain management. Rehabilitation psychologists have also become more involved in public health programs to prevent disabilities, especially those caused by violence and substance abuse. And they testify in court as expert witnesses about the causes and effects of a disability and a person's rehabilitation needs.

School psychologists work directly with public and private schools. They assess and counsel students, consult with parents and school staff, and conduct behavioral intervention when appropriate. Some school districts employ psychologists full time.

Social psychologists study how a person's mental life and behavior are shaped by interactions with other people. They are interested in all aspects of interpersonal relationships, including both individual and group influences, and seek ways to improve such interactions. For example, their research helps us understand how people form attitudes toward others, and when these are harmful—as in the case of prejudice—suggests ways to change them.

Social psychologists are found in a variety of settings, from academic institutions (where they teach and conduct research), to advertising agencies (where they study consumer attitudes and preferences), to businesses and government agencies (where they help with a variety of problems in organization and management).

Sports psychologists help athletes refine their focus on competition goals, become more motivated, and learn to deal with the anxiety and fear of failure that often accompany competition. The field is growing as sports of all kinds become more and more competitive and attract younger children than ever.

THE SUBFIELDS DOCTORAL PSYCHOLOGISTS ENTER

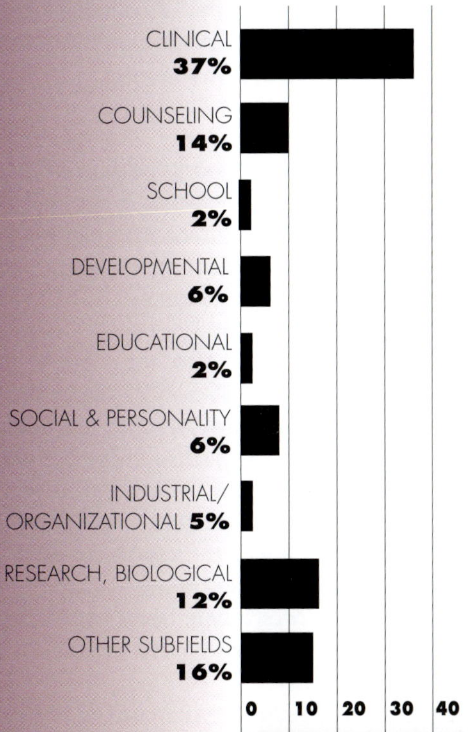

Source: *Summary Report 1997. Doctorate Recipients from U.S. Universities*. Chicago: National Opinion Research Center.

THE JOB OUTLOOK FOR THE NEXT TWO DECADES

Psychology graduates are generally pleased with the way what they studied in school helped prepare them for both life and work. A woman who opened her own business shortly after earning a baccalaureate in psychology explains, "After all, psychology is the business of life." Psychology graduates continue to be excited by the changes taking place in the field that relate to what they are now doing.

The 1997 Doctorate Employment Survey recently compiled by APA's Research Office found that nearly 68 percent of 2,116 psychologists who earned their doctorate in the 1996–1997 academic year secured their first choice when looking for a job. In addition, 69 percent of respondents were employed within 3 months of completing the degree.

The U.S. Bureau of Labor Statistics also has a bright outlook for psychologists. In its 1998–1999 Occupational Outlook Handbook the bureau forecasts that more job opportunities for psychologists will arise in businesses, nonprofit organizations, and research and computer firms for psychologists working as consultants. In addition, the handbook predicts "opportunities for people holding doctorates from leading universities in areas with an applied emphasis, such as clinical, counseling, health and educational psychology, should have particularly good prospects."

Not to say the job market won't be competitive. Many psychologists predict that it will be, and for that reason, Jessica Kohout, PhD, director of APA's Research Office, encourages students to keep their eye on market trends. She foresees that areas such as technology, cultural diversity, and medical delivery will recruit high numbers of psychologists in the coming years.

"Students who are coming out with a knowledge that the market has changed, who work a little harder, and who investigate what those changes are will be in better shape," says Kohout.

Doctoral Graduates

As might be expected, the highest paid and greatest range of jobs in psychology are available to doctoral graduates. Although the number of doctoral graduates has at least doubled over the past 12 years, the demand continues to meet the supply. Furthermore, unemployment and underemployment rates for doctoral psychologists are slightly below the average for other scientists and engineers. Few drop out of the field.

The greatest expansion of career opportunities for doctoral psychologists in the last decade has been in the subfields of clinical, counseling, school, health, industrial, and educational psychology. As a consequence, proportionally fewer new doctorates have headed into faculty positions as compared with the past.

Master's Graduates

The number of psychology students who pursue a terminal master's degree has increased sixfold since 1960. Competition for positions in psychology-related jobs is keen; nevertheless, approximately one-third of those with a master's degree in psychology find such work. Many handle research and data collection and analysis in universities, government, and private companies. Others find jobs in health, industry, and education, the primary work settings for psychology professionals with master's degrees. With growing recognition of the role of psychology in the community, more jobs for persons with master's degrees in psychology may also become available in community mental health centers.

Persons with master's degrees often work under the direction of a doctoral psychologist, especially in clinical, counseling, school, and testing and measurement psychology.

Some jobs in industry, for example, in organizational development and survey research, are held by both doctoral- and master's-level graduates. But industry and government jobs in compensation, training, data analysis, and general personnel issues are often filled by those with master's degrees in psychology.

Bachelor's Graduates

Some students stop with a bachelor's degree in psychology and find work related to their college major. For example, they may be assistants in rehabilitation centers. If they meet state certification requirements, they can teach psychology in high school.

But the study of psychology at the bachelor's level is also a fine preparation for many other professions. In fact, psychology is the second most popular undergraduate major behind business administration. In 1996, about 65,000 college seniors graduated with a degree in psychology, but many were not necessarily interested in a career as a psychologist. Of these 65,000 students, fewer than1 in 10 enrolled in graduate work in psychology. These students often possess good research and writing skills, are good problem solvers, and have well-developed, higher-level thinking ability when it comes to analyzing, synthesizing, and evaluating information. Most find jobs in administrative support, public affairs, education, business, sales, service industries, health, the biological sciences, and computer programming. They work as employment counselors, correction counselor trainees, interviewers, personnel analysts, probation officers, and writers. Two-thirds believe their job is closely or somewhat related to their psychology background and that their jobs hold career potential.

continued

Psychology majors have many qualities that are attractive to job recruiters. Employers find that psychology graduates possess strong people skills. "Once you learn the principles of human behavior," says a banker with a bachelor's degree in psychology, "they're always at the 'top of the mind,' ready to be used. You don't have to stumble across them by accident."

PSYCHOLOGY BA RECIPIENTS SAY THEIR DEGREE RELATES WELL TO THEIR JOB

(% Indicating closely or somewhat related)

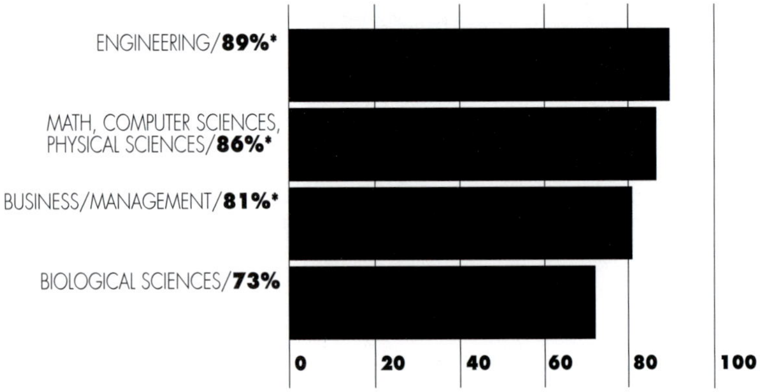

*Significantly higher than average (76%) for total graduates.

Source: U.S. Department of Education, National Center for Education Statistics, 1993 Baccalaureate and Beyond Longitudinal Survey, Second Follow-Up (B & B–93/97), Data Analysis System.

WHERE MOST PSYCHOLOGY BA RECIPIENTS WORK:

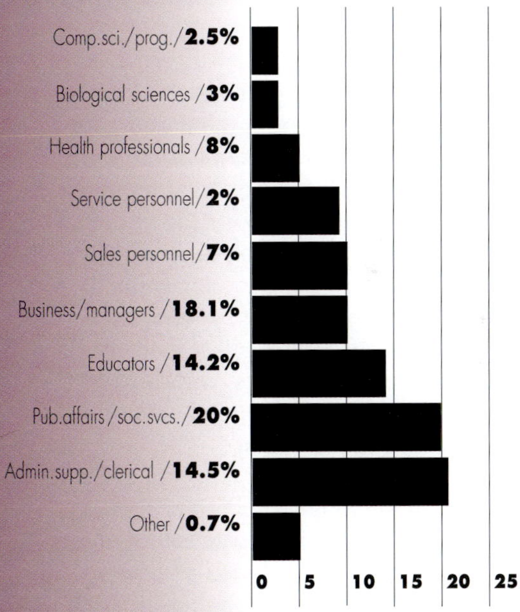

Note: Includes full- and part-time.

WHAT PSYCHOLOGISTS DO AND WHERE THEY DO IT

Psychology is an extraordinarily diverse field with hundreds of career paths. Some specialties, like caring for mentally ill people, are familiar to most of us. Others, like helping with the design of advanced computer systems or studying how we remember things, are less well known.

What all psychologists have in common is a shared interest in mind and behavior, both human and animal. In their work, they draw on an ever-expanding body of scientific knowledge about how we think, act, and feel, and apply the information to their special areas of expertise. Among psychologists, researchers spend most of their time generating knowledge, practitioners apply the knowledge, and some psychologists do both.

In addition to their particular mix of science and practice, psychologists can be distinguished in terms of where they work. Many psychologists work in more than one setting. For instance, college professors often consult for industry or see clients on a part-time basis. Although it's possible to identify a host of different work settings, for the purpose of this booklet, we'll consider some of the most prominent examples.

WHERE DOCTORAL PSYCHOLOGISTS WORK

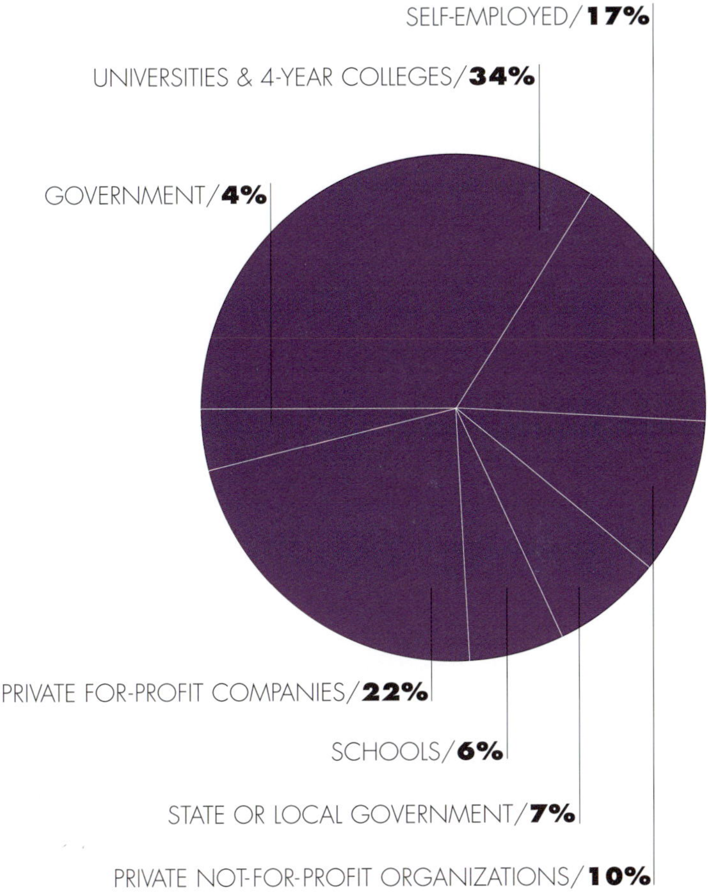

Source: Data for psychologists working full time for others adapted from *1997 Survey of Doctorate Recipients*, National Research Council and National Science Foundation, Washington, D.C. Individual and group practice data are from Research Office, APA Central Programs.

Psychologists Conduct Research

Many psychologists conduct research that runs the gamut from studies of basic brain functions to the behavior of complex social organizations. Subjects of such scientific study include animals, human infants, well-functioning and emotionally disturbed people, elderly people, students, workers, and just about every other population one can imagine. Some research takes place in laboratories where the study conditions can be carefully controlled; some is carried out in the field, such as the workplace, the highway, schools, and hospitals, where behavior is studied as it occurs naturally.

Much of the laboratory research is conducted in universities, government agencies (such as the National Institutes of Health and the armed services), and private research organizations. Whereas most psychological scientists are engaged in the actual planning and conduct of research, some are employed in management or administration—usually after having served as active researchers.

Dr. Alice Eagly is a social psychologist.

My PhD field was social psychology, and one of my special interests is understanding how the social behavior of women and men differs or is similar. At Northwestern University in Evanston, Illinois, I teach an undergraduate course on the psychology of gender and also teach a variety of graduate courses on gender and on the psychology of attitudes.

Gender research is exciting because it deals with intriguing questions about why different groups manifest different behaviors. In my attitude research, I examine people's attitudes, especially toward social issues. Then I look at how attitudes affect people's behavior, the way that they process information, and the way that they resist or are influenced by information that challenges their attitudes. Research on attitudes ultimately helps us understand social problems and social conflict because conflict arises when groups of people have divergent attitudes on important issues.

I've been working on a classic problem in attitude research: the effect of attitudes on memory for attitude-relevant information. Psychologists have long believed that people tend to remember information that agrees with their attitudes. We call this tendency the "congeniality effect." But only some studies have shown this effect, and others have not. Some studies have even shown that people remember uncongenial information better than congenial information. I am trying to disentangle this complex research literature by examining the conditions under which people remember what they agree with or disagree with.

In my gender research, I'm particularly interested in comparing the social behavior of women and men. Are there differences? Are these differences large or small? Of course psychologists have a variety of ideas about the ways in which differences may be due to genetic or cultural causes. So we are trying to test such theories of sex differences scientifically.

Recently I have looked at studies that examined the leadership styles of men and women. We found that to some extent, women tend to be more democratic and participative in leading others. Men tend to be more directive and autocratic. Thus a man might be more likely to tell people what to do. A woman might say, "Well, let's discuss how we should go about doing this and let's also get other opinions."

I am always learning. Students bring new interests into the classroom all the time, and I respond to those interests. And the field of psychology itself is rapidly evolving. New methods, new ways of doing things, and new research questions are always coming up. Life does not get boring if you have an opportunity to always be learning.

Dr. Toni Wegner is a social psychologist.

One of the best things about the field of psychology is that it's so broad. It applies to just about every facet of our lives. Students often take one psych course and find that they really enjoy it. Then they want to take another one and another. Soon they've taken almost enough courses for a major!

Right now I am the director of undergraduate studies for the Department of Psychology at the University of Virginia. We have some psychology students who initially aren't interested in the so-called people-courses. Some, for example, are pre-med majors who at first want to study only the neuromechanisms of behavior.

Once they start taking the other psych courses, however, many become fascinated with how everything ties together.There's no real prerequisite for studying psychology except an interest in learning about people, being able to communicate (not only in writing but also verbally), and having analytical skills.

I earned my undergraduate degree in psychology on an ROTC scholarship at Trinity University. My doctorate is in social psychology from the University of Texas in Austin. After graduate school I joined the Air Force as a personnel research psychologist. We developed tests to determine who would be successful in the military and which people would be better for what jobs. The research skills I had learned as a graduate student were exactly what I needed for that job.

My first job after I left the Air Force was with a company that develops and publishes hundreds of different tests including intelligence tests, aptitude tests, and speech and hearing tests. One of the things I liked most was interacting with a lot of different people and, at the same time, using my knowledge of psychology to solve problems.I then took a Civil Service job at the headquarters for the Air Force Commissary Service, which was, in essence, a grocery store chain. I worked as an industrial/organizational psychologist, that is, someone who applies psychology to the workplace. I was on a project to figure out the best way to select managers for the stores, and I also did surveys on customer satisfaction. I loved using the principles, tools, and research methods of psychology to make decisions that can affect people's lives.

When you major in psychology as an undergraduate, you first take an interesting range of courses in areas such as child psychology, cognition, personality, and social psychology. In your third year you take the methods class and get the tools and proper techniques to be able to think like a psychologist. For the final methods class project, students come up with research ideas, conduct the research, analyze the results, and present the findings to the class on a poster. In this way, they learn how psychologists communicate with each other professionally because psychologists traditionally use "poster sessions" to explain and display their work.

Many people think that university faculty just teach or spend hours in research. But in every job I've had, I've spent most of my time moving around, talking to people, and solving problems. I am fortunate that my profession allows me to be actively involved in the world, which is my style.

Dr. Stanley Sue is a clinical psychologist.

I'm a professor of clinical psychology at the University of California, Los Angeles, and director of the National Research Center on Asian American Health. Unlike psychologists who specialize in a technique or a theory, I specialize in a population. Much of my work focuses on Asian American clients, who often have special needs, especially if they are immigrants from the old country.

I went to an all-boys technical high school wanting to be a television repairman. Within a year, I became disinterested in electronics and woodworking, so I switched schools and tried to prepare myself for college. Along the way, I decided I wanted to become a clinical psychologist even though I was quite naive and didn't know what a clinical psychologist actually did. But I remember always watching a television program called *The Eleventh Hour* that featured both a psychiatrist and a psychologist, and thinking that this is what I wanted to do.

I told my father that I was interested in psychology, particularly clinical psychology. He's Chinese from the old country and couldn't understand what a psychologist does and how one could make a living at it. But I persisted and went to the University of Oregon to major in psychology and then to the University of California at Los Angeles for graduate work. Since then, my three brothers have gone into psychology. The oldest brother even married a psychologist!

At the research center, we're conducting about 20 projects. One is a major study of the rates of mental illness among Chinese people in the United States. Little is known about Asian Americans in this regard. Many people have been saying that Chinese and other Asian Americans don't have many mental health problems. But we know that they have problems just like any other group of people, although there are some differences in the distribution of disorders.

What we have found generally, however, is that Asian Americans tend to underutilize mental health services and that those who do use the services are very disturbed. This means that Asian American people with mild disturbances tend not to come in until their problems are serious.

We're also trying to determine the factors related to mental disturbances among some Chinese people in this country and the factors that seem to insulate others in this population from mental problems. Several researchers at the center are also studying parent–child conflicts in Asian American families to see if the conflicts are different from those affecting other ethnic families and to identify ways to resolve the conflicts. Other investigators are looking at husband–wife problems to ascertain if they're unique because of cultural differences. One researcher has developed a scale that measures "loss of face," which is a particularly important concept for people of Asian descent; fear of losing face affects how they behave. We are also going to look at how much mental health services cost for each ethnic group in our county.

We've seen that Asian Americans tend to drop out of treatment when they see therapists who are not ethnically similar, particularly if the patient has limited proficiency in English. It is one of the reasons we need to diversify the work force. If you're an Asian American who is comfortable in the American culture, you can see a Caucasian therapist, you can see an African American, you can see any therapist. But if you're very traditional or you've just come from overseas, you should have the option of seeing an Asian American therapist.

Psychologists Work in the Community

Work in the community draws a wide range of psychologists. They advise our human services, court, prison, and youth services systems. They also design programs for Boys' and Girls' Clubs, Ys, and community centers.

Some psychologists working in the community study the behavior of adult and juvenile law offenders and develop methods of modifying their behavior. They diagnose and counsel youthful offenders to bring about important behavior changes that keep these offenders out of prison. They provide counseling services within jails or other correctional facilities so that inmates can return to society with better coping skills. They also work in the legal system.

Dr. Pamela Trotman Reid is a developmental psychologist.

Developmental psychologists look at the changes that occur across an entire lifetime. It is a fantastic area because you can do so many different things. You can focus on language development, for example, and study why children's speech may not reflect their thinking. You can look at adolescents and the problems they have in establishing identity. Or you can examine families, from how they use discipline to how they develop attitudes.

There is also a growing interest in adult development and aging, partly because of the graying of America and partly because we are beginning to realize that we don't stop growing when we reach puberty. Instead, we continue to change and develop in many areas all our lives. Developmental psychologists can investigate adult learning issues at the work place, or the effects of aging on cognition.

I was always interested in science; even as a child I had played with chemistry sets. At Howard University in Washington, DC, I majored in chemistry and thought about becoming a medical doctor. But because so many of my friends were taking psychology as an elective, I did, too. Psychology, I learned, is about both science and the application of science to people. I fell in love with the subject, switched my major to psychology, and then went to graduate school and earned my doctorate in educational psychology.

Today, as a researcher and a professor in psychology at the Graduate School and University Center of the City University of New York, I specialize in social development, with my primary interest in the effect of children's gender and culture. I get a great deal of pleasure from teaching and research.

In some of my studies, I have studied why girls act in certain ways and why boys behave in different ways. One small body of research had suggested that women and girls are typically more interested in babies than men and boys are. But all this research had been conducted on White children and adults.

So I looked at both Black and White children, and found no difference between African American boys and girls! In 8- to 10-year-old middle-class children, the White girls liked the babies (they looked at them, touched them, and smiled at them); the African American girls liked the babies; and even the African American boys liked the babies. Only the White boys appeared uninterested in the babies. As often happens, the research led to more questions. Now instead of asking why girls are more interested than boys in babies, the question became, Are we socializing White boys so that they don't like babies?

Currently I'm doing research with children who live in shelters because their parents are homeless. I'm learning about the stresses they undergo so that, perhaps, we can help them learn how some children cope and others do not. For me, the important thing is that in psychology, you can research the questions that you are interested in, not only those that someone else has posed.

Dr. Daniel Abrahamson is a clinical psychologist.

It's important to pick a career that suits your temperament and your likes and dislikes. I grew up in a family that values helping people who are less fortunate and less able to take care of themselves. So psychology was a natural choice for me. I studied clinical psychology in graduate school.

I also went into psychology because I thought it would provide more variety than any other field I'm aware of. I am an administrator, consultant, and researcher.I see patients, work in the community, and am involved with professional groups such as the American Psychological Association. Furthermore, I am surrounded by colleagues who share my excitement.

At the Traumatic Stress Institute, a private health organization in South Windsor, Connecticut, which I helped found, we deal with trauma—everything from natural disasters and industrial accidents to physical and sexual abuse. The institute is a new kind of model for independent practice because we do more than sit in an office for 50 minutes of psychotherapy with a patient—although we do that, too. But we also do research, training, and community education to help traumatized individuals get their lives back on track as quickly as possible. We reassure people who experience trauma that their responses are normal so that they don't think they're going crazy. If it's a young person, we might also work with teachers and administrators in the schools.

We advocate for public policy that provides services and secures rights for those who have experienced traumatic events. We work with the legal system to help people get disability and victim's assistance. One of our psychologists is involved in forensic work, helping judges and attorneys sort out issues about traumatic events that are not always clear-cut in the courtroom. For example, why might someone delay the reporting of a rape or other violent crime?

We also develop psychological measures to try to understand the impact of trauma on the lives of individuals, families, and communities. And we research the types of treatments that are most effective.

In terms of prevention, we work with businesses smart enough to realize that a traumatic situation, such as an industrial accident, can occur. In such cases, we prepare the key people in the organization to respond in a way that not only reduces the immediate impact of the situation but also the long-term consequences.

Five years from now, I hope I'll be doing more work on the significant problems in the working world. As companies modernize and prepare for the 21st century, psychologists can help them figure out how to treat people in a way that allows them to maintain their dignity and to keep themselves productive members of the work world. In this way we can avoid some really serious problems in corporate America.

I can't think of a single part of our culture, a single part of the world that we live in, where psychology doesn't have something to contribute. I get excited when I think that I can make a difference in somebody's life. I love the field.

Dr. Miguel Ybarra is a counseling psychologist.

There are many different ways to come into the field of psychology, but the best way is to understand what your strengths are and what it is you want to accomplish. In my case, I started my academic career as a music major (piano/performance). One of my professors helped me see that my strengths, however, were in another area. I decided that there had to be a better fit for me in a different place. One day I suddenly recognized the fact that people often came to me to talk things out. I felt I had a natural ability to help people see the options that were before them. It was at that moment that I decided to explore what I could get out of (and offer) the field of psychology.

An intimidating prospect that would be required of me, however, was having to master statistics and research methodology. In fact, the very idea of having to learn this material was so frightening, that I almost decided not apply to graduate school at all! The best part of graduate school, however, was that once I started learning the material, it made sense because these "skills" had a real-life application. They became tools that I would use in actually providing the services for which I was training. This was the "best part" of my academic experience because the very thing that almost kept me out of a graduate program became the means to achieve my goals.

During my coursework in counseling psychology at the University of Wisconsin-Madison, I was fortunate enough to work with one of my professors and participate in a study he was directing. The design of this inquiry was to help us learn about the various coping strategies middle school students who live and interact in a multicultural environment use. In other words, we wanted to learn what students do to reduce stress when they are in a setting that is culturally diverse. This experience became even more important to me when I realized that we were also searching for ways to get our findings back to the community that was participating in the study. With great enthusiasm, we presented our findings to the parents and teachers of these students at an open meeting.

Through all of this, I learned that the need for psychologists to bring cross-cultural considerations and multicultural competency to their work is increasing daily because of the changing cultural and ethnic composition of our country. As members of the larger and increasingly diverse society, we need to meet the needs of people from different backgrounds and communities, thus allowing them to build on their strengths. Also, let us not forget the role of language. We must understand the context from which language (and behavior) emanates in order to be successful psychologists, whether we are conducting research, teaching, or providing therapy.

As the field of psychology evolves, we continue to realize how important it is to be inclusive of diversity in terms of ethnicity, culture, gender, sexual orientation, and age (to name just a few). Personally, it is important to me to contribute not only to the field of psychology and to society, but also to my community. I am currently in my second year of teaching in the Counseling Program at Barry University in Miami Shores, FL. In the future, I see myself continuing to help students become quality researchers and educators. I also will continue to give back to the community from which I come; that is, by helping other Latinos/Chicanos, like me, achieve their goals.

Dr. Rodney Hammond is a health psychologist.

I had always wanted to work in the community on real-world problems. As a health psychologist focusing on violence, I can do that.

When I started as an undergraduate at the University of Illinois, Champaign-Urbana, I hadn't decided on my major. But, to help finance my education, I took a part-time job in a child development research program sponsored by the psychology department. There, I observed young inner-city children in settings designed to enhance their learning. I saw first-hand the contributions psychology can make, and I knew I wanted to be a psychologist.

After completing undergraduate work in psychology, I went on to earn my doctorate, focusing on children, both in school and in the community. When I graduated, there was no such thing as a health psychologist. I started as an assistant professor in a doctoral program in school psychology at the University of Tennessee. But soon, I went on to direct a children's program at Meharry Medical College in Nashville. As a psychologist in a medical setting, I could help children with health problems and also help their families and the physicians who worked with them.

At Meharry, I was in charge of an extensive and innovative program with an interdisciplinary staff. We worked with children who had developmental disabilities, dealt with child abuse and neglect, developed partial hospitalization for children with emotional problems, and created prevention programs for youth at risk. Following that position, I became assistant dean at the Wright State University School of Professional Psychology in Ohio, where I trained clinical psychologists and directed a program, PACT (Positive Adolescent Choices Training) to prevent homicide and violence among minority youth.

Today, I am the director of the Division of Violence Prevention, National Center for Injury Prevention and Control of the Centers for Disease Control and Prevention (CDC). Through the Division of Violence Prevention, I oversee the work of the CDC to prevent injuries and deaths caused by violence. The division, with its budget of more than $90 million, manages research, surveillance, and programs in intentional injury; homicide; suicide; youth, family, and intimate partner violence prevention; and rape and sexual assault prevention.

As director of this CDC division, I oversee the world's largest contingent of public health experts and scientists in the world working on violence issues and prevention. These experts and scientists work in a variety of fields, including medicine, sociology, anthropology, criminology, and epidemiology. I am also involved in global efforts to prevent violence through the World Health Organization and Pan-American Health Organization.

Through my work, I've been able to achieve a career level unprecedented by a psychologist—I am the first psychologist to serve as the director of a division of the Centers for Disease Control and Prevention. As you can see from my experience and background, my early work as a health psychologist was the basis for, but just the beginning of, this adventure. Psychology is much more than the traditional roles you may be aware of. When you think of a career in psychology, think beyond those limited roles!

Psychologists Help People Learn

Psychologists provide a number of services—both direct and indirect—to children, youth, and families in schools at all levels, from nursery school through college. Many focus on improving the effectiveness of teaching and student learning, frequently by studying motivation and cognitive processes in the classroom.

School psychologists also provide counseling and crisis intervention services. They help students with learning or behavior problems, learning disabilities, and cognitive deficits. They work with students in schools to prevent violence and other disruptive behaviors. They also serve on interdisciplinary teams that develop individual educational plans for students with special needs. Psychologists work within specialty areas of learning, too, such as the arts and sports.

Dr. Sylvia Rosenfield is a school psychologist.

A school psychologist has one of the most varied jobs I know of. I am currently a professor in the school psychology program at the University of Maryland in College Park. During my career, I have also been a school psychologist in Madison, Wisconsin, and worked with public schools in several states. I've been a faculty member at Fordham University in New York and at Temple University in Pennsylvania. And I've had the opportunity to work with state education departments and with school systems around the country. (If you like to travel, psychology isn't a bad career!) My doctorate is in educational psychology, with a specialty in school psychology.

It is important to me to be out of the university occasionally and go into the public schools. For example, I am working with the Howard County school system to change the way schools work with children who have learning and behavior problems.

Students who come into the graduate program in school psychology have usually gained an understanding about human behavior and about the way people interact with their environments from their undergraduate psychology courses. Graduate courses in school psychology provide advanced study on applying research findings in the real world, so you can help teachers, school administrators, and parents understand how children learn, develop, and are motivated.

One of the courses I teach is on consultation skills, taken in the second year of our graduate program in school psychology. Students spend a whole year working with teachers on solving problems in the classroom. Each week the student and I listen to tapes of those discussions to make certain that the student is acquiring the skills critical to a school psychologist.

I can remember when computers were in basements of huge university buildings. Now they're in many classrooms and most schools. We're using them to keep track of information about children and their academic achievements. Also, we use them to get information. For example, if you have a child with a particular kind of problem in one school, you can use a computer network to find information about this type of problem or to talk to psychologists in other places through e-mail and computer bulletin boards.

School psychology is one of the oldest areas of applied psychology. It's based on the scientific-practitioner model, which means that our practice has a scientific base and we use the scientific method in our work. There is a school psychologist in almost every school in America. And that's one of the real contributions psychology is making to American children.

We apply what we know—about learning, instruction, motivation, growth and development, and interpersonal relationships—in the school setting. We work with adults and children, so we have to have good interpersonal skills, as well. The school psychologist can help create healthy environments where children and youth can flourish.

Everybody has spent a large part of his/her life in school. But when you come back as a school psychologist, you see the schools in a new way. You have the opportunity to find ways to make them better places for children and for teachers.

Dr. Todd Gravois is a school psychologist.

We've all had this perception of psychology as a couch-profession, so it's nice to be able to tell people that psychologists are found in many fields. School psychology is an area that students oftentimes overlook, but when they see the valuable contribution it makes to the field of education, they become enthusiastic.

I work predominantly with elementary school students, kindergarten through fifth grade, in Howard County, Maryland. I like being a school psychologist because I value education and I value giving people equal opportunities to get that education.

There has been a lot of research in school psychology that we use when we work with children and adults. And we evaluate our work scientifically so we can demonstrate whether it's effective or not.

School psychologists need to understand how organizations work and be able to work with a multitude of people: teachers, school psychologists, guidance counselors, and administrators, each with his or her own strengths. The Howard County school system and the University of Maryland have created a program to train these professionals in collaborating as teams.

Computers are an important tool for school psychologists. They help us analyze the data we collect. We also use them when talking with children about things that are going on in their lives. Children today are often more comfortable with computers than they are with paper and pencil.

Psychologists Promote Physical and Mental Health

Psychologists as health providers span a large and diverse spectrum of subfields. Today, many psychologists work alone, with patients and clients coming to the psychologist's office.

Increasingly, however, psychologists in independent practice are contracting on either a part-time or a full-time basis with organizations to provide a wide range of services. For example, a psychologist can join a health practice and work with a team of other health care providers, such as physicians, nutritionists, physiotherapists, and social workers to prevent or treat illness. This team approach, which is likely to become more common in the future, frequently includes efforts to change unhealthy behaviors and ensure that patients follow the recommended treatment. The team also helps patients cope with stress.

Psychologists also instruct students who are training to become health care professionals, such as physicians and nurses, about the psychological factors involved in illness. And they advise health care providers already in practice about the psychological bases of much illness so that symptoms that are psychological in origin can be better diagnosed and treated.

Psychologists involved in health care teams typically work in hospitals, medical schools, outpatient clinics, nursing homes, pain clinics, rehabilitation facilities, and community health and mental health centers.

Dr. Carol Manning is a neuropsychologist.

My doctoral degree was in clinical psychology. I do clinical work, research, and teaching at the University of Virginia. All three aspects of my career are very important to me.

For example, I work in a memory disorders clinic as part of a team of neurologists, nurses, and medical technicians. I oversee patient treatment apart from medication. What I learn in my research, I use in my clinical practice. And in my clinical practice, I learn the important questions to ask in my research.

One of my patients who has Alzheimer's disease is in a clinical drug trial involving an experimental medication. No one knows if he is receiving medication or a placebo, which is something that looks like the medication but actually isn't anything at all.

I assess this gentleman periodically and also talk with his wife occasionally to determine whether his condition has changed. I test his ability to remember things, and I look to see if the kinds of judgments he makes are the same kinds of judgments you or I would make. I test his ability to know the time and the date and the place—to see if he knows generally where he is. I look at his ability to copy drawings and also to remember those drawings. I also check his attention span.

Computers are becoming increasingly important in all kinds of science, including psychology. A lot of psychology now involves programming models to understand the networks of the brain. I use computers to run experiments. This morning I tested a patient's spatial memory, where he had to remember where words were placed on the screen. I also use computers for statistics—to figure out what my data means.

I teach in the Department of Neurology, and some of my work involves supervising graduate students. It's most important that my students are truly interested in psychology and in the projects they're working on. They need to think creatively, they need to be determined, and they need to work thoroughly and carefully.

I'm helping one graduate student learn to do therapy and to assess patients. Another graduate student works with me on research studies. She helps me guide people through the research program on the computer. She analyzes data, and she's learned to do statistics and how to design studies. We write papers together for publication.

If you're interested in psychology, I'd advise you to take psychology courses as an undergraduate. And try to work in a research laboratory so that you can get some insight into what the field is really like.

Many of today's students are encouraged to take time off between undergraduate and graduate school because it's a long haul and it takes a lot of determination. Sometimes I think it's nice for people to have a break in there. It takes persistence to earn a doctorate in psychology, along with a great interest in psychological research, science, and people. It takes a long time—but I think it's well worth it!

Dr. Barbara A. Brauer is a clinical psychologist.

I was born in Evanston, Illinois, the oldest of three children. Apparently, I was born deaf. We don't know what caused it. There is no deafness in the family records, and my sister and brother both hear.

When I was about two and a half years old, I was sent to the Lutheran School for the Deaf, in Detroit. When my parents thought that I had learned all I could there, they enrolled me in the Evanston public school system. Thus I was mainstreamed into the sixth grade at the age of 10.

It worked out beautifully for me. The first year I had a special education assistant to help me make the transition. One of the first things that struck me was that I was getting a far superior education than at a school for the deaf.

After the first year, I was on my own. I now wonder how I ever did it. It wasn't too bad when I was in high school because most of the lectures were in the textbooks. In college, however, much of what the professors were saying was not in the texts. There were no interpreters in those days, so I'd borrow my classmates' notes and type them up fast so I could return them. (It was before there were photocopy machines!)

In a high school civics class, I saw some films about possible professions, and psychiatry caught my eye. However because medical schools in those days did not admit deaf people, I decided to go into psychology. I got a master's in counseling from Columbia University, a doctorate in educational psychology from New York University, and did an internship in clinical psychology at Saint Elizabeth's Hospital in Washington, DC.

Today, there are about 25 deaf psychologists in the country. I was one of the first three "pioneers," and also the first deaf woman to become a psychologist. I worked for 12 years in a unit for deaf people at St. Elizabeth's Hospital, where I did individual, group, and family therapy, and program evaluation. Then I came to the mental health research program at Gallaudet University; Gallaudet is the only 4-year liberal arts college in the world for people who are deaf or hard of hearing.

In addition to teaching, I also did research at Gallaudet on translating paper-and-pen types of psychological tests into sign language for videotape format so that deaf people can take these tests on computers anywhere. (Four tests have been translated.) Deaf people, by and large, cannot read at the level required to understand the questions on the psychological test, especially the idioms. For example, one test has a question that asks: "Do you sometimes feel like you are all thumbs?" Deaf people don't understand that question.

After 14 years, I moved into administration and now direct the Community Counseling and Mental Health Clinic at Gallaudet. This clinic, the first of its kind, was established primarily to train deaf students in counseling and clinical psychology.

A psychologist doesn't have to be deaf to work well with deaf clients, but must master sign language and know about and understand deafness, deaf people, and deaf culture. By the same token, it is not easy for a student who is deaf to become a psychologist because mastery of the English language is required, particularly to write a thesis. It is only in recent years that some clinical psychology programs have started admitting deaf students. But there is a big demand for psychologists to work with the deaf, and jobs are available.

Dr. Lynn Rehm is a clinical psychologist.

I always had an interest in science. As a math major at the University of Southern California, I worked on a research project using some fairly complex mathematical and statistical approaches to try to understand the nature of intelligence. I liked the idea of applying mathematics to complex human problems.

I decided to do my doctoral work in clinical psychology partly because the field is so broad; there are roles for clinical psychologists in virtually every setting. I like that. For example, I see patients and also supervise graduate students who see patients. I also teach abnormal psychology at the University of Houston and work with graduate students on their research.

In addition, I do research. It's exciting to design a project, study a problem, reap the data, and then be able to look at the numbers and detect a pattern. Such research helps us better understand what we're doing in treatment and the nature of various kinds of problems that people have.

My particular interest is clinical depression: how it occurs, who develops depression and why, and how the illness can be treated. Clinical depression involves more than just feeling blue. It's a change in mood that won't go away and interferes with daily functioning. Some of the symptoms are fatigue, loss of appetite, difficulty in sleeping, and loss of interest in sex.

Depression has its roots in a person's psychological and biological make-up as well as in the person's environment. Depression is a common problem and one that many people don't recognize, even though they themselves may be severely depressed or living or working with a depressed person.

I have also become interested in how to detect depression in different settings. I've worked with school children to try to prevent depression. I've consulted with staff at a correctional facility to set up a depression treatment program for prisoners. I'm now working in a Veterans' Administration hospital, where we look at depression in posttraumatic stress disorder.

I've developed a therapy program that takes a cognitive–behavioral approach to help people overcome depression by teaching them about the nature of depression itself and how to change some of the pieces that make up the disorder.

I find working with depression rewarding because this mood disorder is eminently treatable. You see changes in patients, in their outlook on life, and in their view of themselves. It's great, for example, to see the return of a sense of humor in a patient because it is often one of the best indicators that he or she is getting better.

Depression also has an effect on loved ones who want so much to offer help and encouragement but find it frustrating and difficult to live with a depressed person. So when a patient improves, you also see gratifying changes in the whole family.

Psychologists Study and Contribute to the Work Environment

Anywhere people work, and anything they do while at work, is of interest to psychologists. Psychologists study what makes people effective, satisfied, and motivated in their jobs; what distinguishes good workers or managers from poor ones; and what conditions of work promote high or low productivity, morale, and safety.

Some psychologists design programs for recruiting, selecting, placing, and training employees. They evaluate, monitor, and improve performance. They help make changes in the way the organization is set up.

Others help design the actual tasks, tools, and environments with which people must deal when doing their jobs. These specialists can also help design the products that organizations turn out and conduct research related to product design. For example, they play a big role in making computer hardware and software more user-friendly, which in turn contributes both to operator performance in the workplace and product acceptability in the marketplace.

Psychologists with training in mental health and health care also deal with the health and adjustment of individuals in the work setting. They work with employee assistance plans that provide help with drug or alcohol addiction problems, depression, and other disorders; they also foster healthy behavior.

Dr. David Sirota is an industrial/organizational psychologist.

When I began my career as an industrial/organizational psychologist there was an emphasis on testing—ability testing, personality testing, and so on—in an effort to put the right person in the right job. Today, the emphasis is turning to establishing the atmosphere most conducive to productivity and quality work.

The field has become extremely influential, in part because of the overwhelming competition from Japan. Studies indicate that Japanese companies tend to manage the way industrial/organizational psychologists say people should be managed.

Most industrial/organizational psychologists hold that people go to work wanting to do good work. Nevertheless, when we look at a company that has a problem—let's say, a drop in customers or a large turnover in labor—we see large percentages of people not working very hard. When we analyze what causes people to lose their motivation, the answer usually has to do with how they're being managed. For example, if management treats employees like children or criminals, the employees are likely to become demoralized.

I had wanted to be a psychologist since I was a psychology major at City College of New York. (I originally thought I would go into engineering.) One great influence on me was my father. He was a strong union man. From him I learned that workers' opinions are very important to a company's overall well-being. While earning my doctorate in social psychology at the University of Michigan, I also became enamored of survey work at the university's Institute for Social Research.

I was an industrial/organizational psychologist for IBM for 13 years and then set up my own consulting firm, Sirota and Associates, in New York City. We do work for companies all over the world. Earlier in my career, I also taught at a number of universities.

My particular branch of the field focuses on data collection. We diagnose an organization's problems by surveying people in the organization through questionnaires, informal interviews, focus groups, or a combination of all three methods. Why do employees stay with the company? What helps them produce quality products or quality service? Do they have the right training, the right equipment, the right management, the right whatever? Does the way management treats employees cause them to feel good or bad about the company's customers? Often we interview the customers, too. All these variables comprise the heart of what we do.

We come back to management with our analysis. We try to be candid, but not abrasive, pointing out what's being done well and the opportunities for improvement. We then try to get the managers involved in coming to their own solutions.

Unlike a doctor who finds out what's wrong with you and then writes a prescription, most industrial/organizational psychologists want people to become their own doctors. We're not necessarily interested in people liking each other or becoming "nice guys," per se. Of course, it's good if they do, but what we want is for them to deal with what has to be done in terms of business objectives.

GETTING READY TO WORK IN PSYCHOLOGY

If you are interested in a career as a psychologist, you have to complete graduate school with a major in psychology. While most academic departments offering such a major are located in the university colleges of arts and sciences, some are also located in professional schools of psychology, education, business, medicine, and engineering.

Take time to research your choices. The program should match your interests. Although most psychology departments offer a breadth of education in the discipline of psychology, they vary in their strengths or areas of emphasis. You need to find out what those are and match them to your graduate education interests. The areas of expertise and research interests of individual faculty members can be a guide to you in matching your career interest with a specific area of research or practice in psychology.

A graduate or professional school's catalogue, brochures, and Web site are generally the best and most current sources of information about the nature of each graduate program and its program and admission requirements. A composite source of such information is available also in the American Psychological Association (APA) publication Graduate Study in Psychology. *That can be ordered through the APA via e-mail: order@apa.org; telephone: (800) 374-2721; or at the Web site: apa.org.*

Throughout the application process, discuss your plans with an advisor or your undergraduate faculty. Apply to a number of programs that offer you a reasonable chance of acceptance. For more information, you may contact the APA Education Directorate at 750 First Street, N.E., Washington, DC 20002; e-mail: education@apa.org; or Web site: apa.org/about/contact.html.

If you are interested in a career in psychology, take time to research your choices. The program you select should match your interests. For example, some psychology departments may specialize in a subfield of psychology that appeals to you. Also investigate the areas of expertise and research interests of individual faculty members.

High School Preparation

A strong college preparatory high school education is a good beginning for a career in psychology. Courses in science, math, English, history, social studies, and a foreign language are important. Science and math are particularly important because they provide the necessary skills for research and analysis in college psychology courses. Some high schools offer a course in psychology, which can give you an overview of what the field is about. You can also find a volunteer job where psychologists work, or read about psychology in newspapers and magazines to explore the field. Do not be misguided, however, by popular stereotypes of the field. Psychology is a broad behavioral science with many applications.

Bachelor's Degree

Most undergraduate programs require a blend of science and liberal arts courses for a bachelor's degree in psychology. The courses usually include introductory psychology, experimental psychology, and statistics. Other required courses can be in learning, personality, abnormal psychology, social psychology, developmental psychology, physiological or comparative psychology, history and systems, and tests and measurement. Typically, you will be ready to take electives in psychology by the time you are a college junior. It is a good time to make graduate school plans so you can make wise choices about future courses and extracurricular activities during the last 2 years of college. Know, however, that as long as you've taken some electives in psychology, you don't always need to have a bachelor's in psychology to get into a graduate program in the field.

The Value of the Undergraduate Degree

Psychology majors, whether they have gone on to careers in psychology (the majority do not) or other fields, cite courses in the principles of human behavior as especially important to life after college. The additional insight gained from these courses into what motivates people to perform at their peak helps them, whether they are functioning as parents at home, managers on the job, or professionals in other fields.

Many bachelor's degree holders credit their college psychology courses with teaching them how people, including themselves, learn. "I use information on learning reinforcement every time I conduct a training session for my employees," says a manager in a consumer products company.

Above all, it is the rigorous training in the scientific method—the need to do thorough, objective research, analyze data logically, and put forth the findings with clarity—that stands psychology majors in good stead as they pursue their future careers.

GRADUATE SCHOOL

Most graduate departments require that you take a standard aptitude test, usually the Graduate Record Examination (GRE). Although programs vary in the weight they attach to test scores, successful applicants typically score well above 500 on both the verbal and quantitative portions of the GRE. Determine if your GRE scores will qualify you for consideration by the institution to which you would like to apply. Competition for spaces in graduate school is keen.

Master's Degree

Undergraduate course requirements for a terminal master's degree are relatively few: usually, a background in introductory or general psychology, experimental psychology with a laboratory course, and statistics. The university usually takes the undergraduate grade point average (GPA) into account, too.

A recent survey of 26 psychology master's programs shows that the most commonly required courses once you are in the master's program are those with industrial/organizational content, statistics, and research design. Course work at the master's level often also includes study in ethics, assessment, program evaluation, and personality related topics as well.

A master's degree in psychology, along with preparation in the natural sciences or mathematics, is increasingly valued by doctoral programs in psychology. Each doctoral program also decides which credits earned at the master's level it will accept for transfer. Occasionally, students need to repeat some course work. Some institutions will not accept a master's degree from any school other than their own. For these reasons, it is important to ask questions about these and other issues early in the application process.

Doctoral Degree

Each graduate program determines its own entrance requirements. Some doctoral programs require applicants to have a master's degree in psychology. For others, students can enter the doctoral programs with a bachelor's degree and work directly on a doctoral degree.

Earning a doctoral degree typically requires at least 4 years, with the median time to degree being closer to 7 years of study after the bachelor's degree. Early in the graduate program, you will probably take course work in the core areas of psychology. You will work with a professor to learn how to do research; you'll also study how psychological research is applied to life situations. Once you have completed all the course work, you must pass a comprehensive exam and write and defend a dissertation or other scholarly product.

If you want to be a professional psychologist in clinical, counseling, school, or other health service areas of psychology, you will also have to complete a 1-year internship as part of your doctoral study in these areas of practice. You may wish to consider a doctoral program in a professional school rather than at a traditional university. Professional schools typically place greater emphasis on training students for professional practice and less emphasis on research. Some universities and professional schools offer a PsyD degree in lieu of the traditional research doctoral degree PhD. In choosing applicants, these programs may look for candidates who already have clinical experience or other work experience in applied psychology.

The Importance of Accreditation

There are two kinds of accreditation: institutional and specialized. Institutional accreditation certifies that an institution has met minimum standards of quality. It is granted by one of seven regional accrediting organizations recognized for this purpose by the U.S. Department of Education. Membership in the APA requires that one's doctoral degree in psychology or equivalent be from an accredited institution. Most state licensing boards in psychology also have such a requirement, though some require that the licensure applicant have graduated from an accredited doctoral program in psychology. The latter is what we refer to as specialized accreditation.

Specialized accreditation only applies to professional programs. It certifies that the program meets the minimal standards of quality as defined by that profession. In the field of psychology, specialized

NUMBER OF DEGREES AWARDED IN PSYCHOLOGY BY LEVEL OF DEGREE: 1995-1996

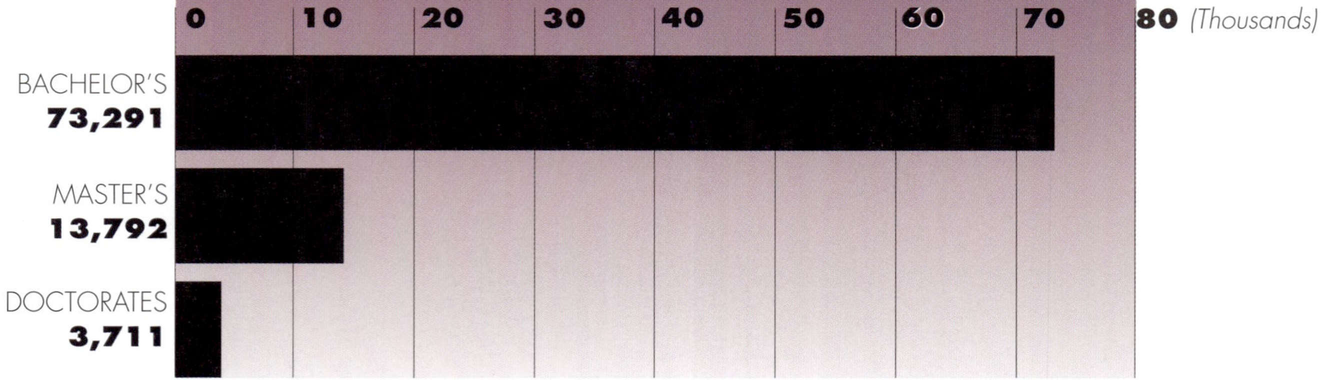

Source: Adapted from U.S. Department of Education, National Center for Education Statistics, Integrated Postsecondary Education Data Systems (IPEDS), "Completions" surveys, Junes 1998.

accreditation is granted by the APA Committee on Accreditation and applies only to doctoral programs, internships and postdoctoral residency programs in health service areas of professional psychology. Increasingly, employers and health services reimbursement companies require that the psychologists whom they employ or reimburse be graduates of accredited programs in professional psychology.

For more information about accredited programs, contact the APA Education Directorate at 750 First Street, N.E., Washington, DC 20002-4242; e-mail: education@apa.org.

If You Need Financial Aid

You may be able to get financial aid to attend both undergraduate and graduate school. Assistance comes in different forms: fellowships, scholarships, grants or subsidies, work study programs, federal loans, and teaching or research assistantships. Graduate assistantships and work study require part-time work.

Students seeking financial aid for a graduate degree should get advice as early as possible. Consult with both the psychology office and the office of financial aid on your own campus and also with the office of financial aid at the school to which you are applying. Students of ethnic minority background should also contact the APA Minority Fellowship Training Program.

Licensure and Certification

For independent practice as a psychologist anywhere in the United States or Canada, you must be licensed or certified for such. Before granting you permission to take the licensing exam, the state licensing board will review your educational background. A doctoral degree does not automatically make you eligible; requirements vary from state to state. At a minimum, states require that the doctorate be in psychology or a field of study "primarily psychological in nature" and that it be from a regionally accredited institution. You also must have had at least 2 years of supervised professional experience. Information about state and provincial licensing/certification requirements can be obtained from the American Association of State and Provincial Psychology Boards (ASPPS) at the following addresses: P.O. Box 4389 Montgomery, AL, 36103 or http://www.asppb.org.

APA RESOURCES FOR STUDENTS

The major organization of psychologists around the world, the American Psychological Association, has worked for more than 100 years to advance psychology as a science, a profession, and a way to promote human welfare. It has more than 160,000 members and affiliates.

Student affiliates

Undergraduate and graduate students taking courses in psychology are eligible for membership in APA as student affiliates. Student affiliates receive free subscriptions to the *American Psychologist* journal and *The APA Monitor on Psychology. The APA Monitor on Psychology* is a monthly magazine that covers the work of the four directorates of APA (Practice, Education, Science, and Public Interest), the impact of psychology on society, and the work of the association and individual members in advocacy and legislative action affecting psychology and behavioral science. The *Monitor* also has an extensive job listing. Student affiliates may purchase APA publications at special rates and attend the APA annual convention at a reduced registration fee.

Graduate student association

All graduate student affiliates of APA are automatically members of the American Psychological Association of Graduate Students (APAGS), created in 1988 as a voice for psychology students within the larger association. (Undergraduates can join APAGS by paying a small additional fee.) APAGS was formed by graduate students as a means of establishing communication between students and other members of the psychological community, including universities, training centers, and other members of the APA governance structure. APAGS represents all graduate study specialties of the discipline and is run by student leaders elected by the APAGS membership. In addition to a variety of other initiatives, the group sponsors programming of the APA annual convention each year and distributes a quarterly newsletter to its members.

Student membership in APA divisions

APA student affiliates are encouraged to apply for affiliation in one or more of APA divisions. The divisions bring together psychologists of similar or specialized professional interests. You can obtain more information about any division listed by contacting the APA Office of Division Services.

Minority Undergraduate Students of Excellence (MUSE)

The MUSE program is administered by the APA Office of Ethnic Minority Affairs. The program provides information on application and financial aid procedures to outstanding minority undergraduate students interested in graduate psychology studies who are selected through a nomination process. For more information, contact the APA Office of Minority Affairs.

Publications

APA publishes about 3 dozen peer-reviewed journals and more than 400 books in the major interest areas in psychology. APA also produces several electronic databases, two of which—PsycINFO® and PsycLIT®—contain abstracts of psychological literature from 1974 to present (also available in most libraries in print form).

To help individuals negotiate the sequence of activities involved in becoming a psychology student and a psychologist, APA has developed a line of books for undergraduate and graduate students as well as those who are just now planning to go to college. *Is Psychology the Major for You?* helps individuals decide on and prepare for an undergraduate major in psychology. Students interested in graduate school find that *Getting In: A Step-by-Step Guide to Gaining Admission to Graduate School in Psychology* helps to guide their decision making, structure the application process, and maximize their chances of being accepted and getting financial aid. *Graduate Study in Psychology and Associated Fields* complements *Getting In* by summarizing more than 600 programs of study in psychology, requirements for admission for each program, deadlines for applications, and other details potential applicants need to know about specific schools.

The *Publication Manual of the American Psychological Association* and *Mastering APA Style: Student's Workbook and Training Guide* help both undergraduate and graduate students with their class papers and, for those who go on to graduate school, prepare them to submit articles to psychological journals. The *Publication Manual* is often required reading for students in psychology and many of the other social sciences. Additional resources to help both undergraduate and graduate students include *Library Use: A Handbook for Psychology, Search PsycINFO: Student Workbook*, and *Journals in Psychology: A Resource Listing for Authors.*

Understanding Multivariate Statistics helps graduate students understand the scientific articles they will be required to read as a major part of their training. Because the book clearly explains which multivariate statistics are most appropriate for which kinds of research questions, it also helps prepare students for graduate statistics courses and for eventually conducting their own research.

Dissertations and Theses From Start to Finish: Psychology and Related Fields gives students essential guidance on what is perhaps the most challenging task of their graduate career. This easy-to-follow book covers such areas as choosing a topic, finding a chairperson for a dissertation or thesis committee, preparing a proposal, designing and conducting the research, writing the dissertation or thesis, and defending it.

Finally, for those who may decide to teach and do research in an academic setting, *The Psychologist's Guide to an Academic Career* offers a realistic yet encouraging look at the academic profession, from preparation in graduate school through tenured service. Becoming a faculty member, an effective teacher, and an ethical researcher; getting published and obtaining grants; and advancing to tenure and being promoted are among the many topics discussed.

Many public and university libraries carry these books. You can also order them or other books from APA's extensive catalog by calling 1–800–374–2721. (In Washington, DC, call 336–5510.)

APA on Internet

PsychNet is APA's home page on the Worldwide Web. It contains information for psychologists, psychology students, media, and the general public. The Internet address is http://www.apa.org.

Student Honor Societies

Psi Chi is the national honor society in the field of psychology. It recognizes excellence in scholarship by graduate and undergraduate psychology students. You can apply for membership through a chapter located at an accredited college or university. To be eligible for membership, undergraduates must rank in the upper 35 percent of their class and must have completed a specified number of credits in psychology. Graduate students must have at least a "B" average. A registration fee pays for a lifetime membership. The *Psi Chi Newsletter* is published quarterly.

Psi Beta is the honor society for psychology students who attend 2-year colleges. In addition to its campus-based activities, Psi Beta operates the Psi Beta Diversity Project 2000, which involves mentoring activities for community college students of color. National office: 407 East 5th Street, Suite B, Chattanooga, TN 37403, (615) 265–6555.

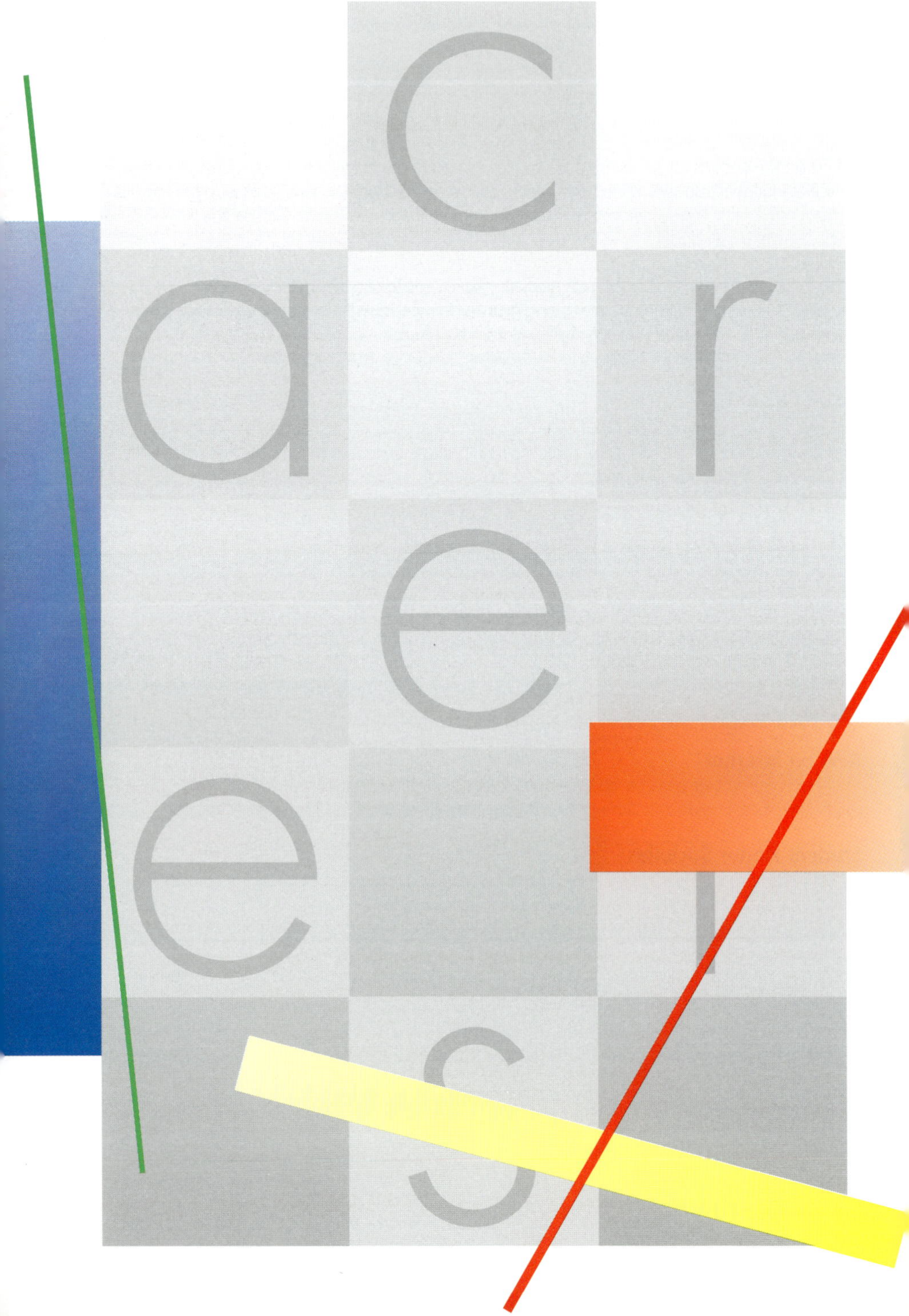

Ordering information

Companion Video:
Psychology: Scientific Problem Solvers—
Careers for the 21st Century.
Closed Captioned for the hearing impaired.
1995.
Time: About 14 minutes.
VHS format.

To order copies of the publication or video of
Psychology: Scientific Problem Solvers—Careers for the 21st Century,
contact the APA order department:

1-800-374-2721.

In Washington, DC, call

(202) 336-5510, (202) 336-6123.

Video only:
APA Member/Affiliate & List: $19.95
Item #4313060

Video and 50 copies of pamphlet:
APA Member/Affiliate & List: $39.95
Item #4313065